The Lord's Prayer

Randall Lechner

The Play

_____

Tiitle: The Lord's Prayer
Author: Randall Lechner
Copyright © Randall Lechner, November, 2017
Published By Parables, November, 2017

All Rights Reserved. No part of this book may be reproduced or utilized in any form or by any means, electronic or mechanical, including photocopying, recording, or by any information storage and retrieval system, without permission in writing from the author.

The cover photos of the KATY Trail taken by the author Randall Lechner.

Unless otherwise specified Scripture quotations are taken from the authorized version of the King James Bible.

    ISBN 978-1-945698-31-6
    Printed in the United States of America

Readers should be aware that Internet Web sites offered as citations and/or sources for further information may have been changed or disappeared between the time this was written and when it is read.

The Lord's Prayer
Randall Lechner
The Play

"The Lord's Prayer"

A play written from the creative inspiration from the Holy Spirit while riding on a short, 15-mile bike on the KATY Trail Nov 19th, 2007.

Scene I

The overhead projection will need 3 screens for the power point projections:

1. One over the left corner angled so the entire audience can see it with ease.
2. The same on the right side of the stage.
3. The main center stage overhead screen positioned behind the narrator, about a minimum of 15 feet, and above him, if possible, about the same, make it proportionate to the size of the stage.

In the center of the stage sits a tan recliner. Beside it is an old 2 tier end table with a small table light. The end table is stacked with 2 Bibles, one is a study Bible, an old version of the New International, and a Maroon colored leather Bible for reading. On top of them are notepads and ink pens.

On the top tier, there is unopened mail and stacks of papers that have yet to be sorted and filed. And a tall plastic glass of water, the glass has the St Louis Cardinals printed on the side of it...a souvenir drink from one of many attended games within the past years. Beside the glass, is a pair of reading glasses.

On the other side of the recliner is a phone stand, and a cabinet door in which to store all kinds of books, papers, etc. On top of the table is a printer cluttered with papers, yet to be copied.

On the tan recliner sits a closed laptop computer, 13", on the left arm (viewed if sitting in the chair facing out).

On the right arm are both a cell phone and the TV remote.

On the back of the recliner is a throw blanket or a lap blanket.

To the back part of the right side of the stage, (view: standing in front of the stage) will be a double-wide door set. Over the top of the door will be a sign, yet to be determined, but with some definite thoughts in mind. It will be illuminated at the end of the play, but not to be noticed during the play. (I have a couple of different endings in mind.)

On both sides of the door will be windows with the looks of bars, similar to a jail, but not as prominent…more suggestive in appearance.

The room is to be designed as though it is a large visiting area in a hospital. To the back left of the room (standing in front of the stage looking toward it), sits a roller office chair with an old computer desk or a small folding table next to it.

A portable swinging arm floor lamp sits beside the reclining chair.

On top of the craft table are a sketch pad with some drawing pencils, a plastic bottle of water, and a pair of bifocal glasses on top of the sketch pad.

Behind the sketch pad, on the table, is a table easel with an unfinished painting of some heavenly clouds.

Behind the chair, on the wall, is an oil painting and some pictures of 3 grown children and their families.

The area is to be designed like a room in a nursing home or semi-retired assisted living room. A door to represent going into the room should be stage left of the chair. There will be a small sign hanging over the door, but not sure just what it will say, but it will be illuminated at the end of the play.

Standing in front of the stage, viewing to the left will be a nursery room designed for a young mother and 6-month-old baby.

The room décor is of animals and not too girly.

Also, for the girl's part in the play, there is a twin bed with an older girl about age 5. She is in her P.J.s and lying on her bed, watching her mother get the baby ready for bed.

The young mother is acting as if she is speaking to both the baby and the 5-year-old daughter in a dimly lit setting, just enough to allow the balance of the stage to be seen, but not distract from the main act that is taking place.

The same for the opposite side of the stage when the young mother is being highlighted and when the middle of the stage is spotlighting the narrator's act.

Standing in front of the stage, viewing the front right, will be a bedroom setting for a boy about the age of 10-12.

This is a bedroom scene of a much younger father with his son, (the same age group as the young mother).

You can see a nightstand, next to the young boy's single twin bed, that is angled as if in the corner of his room, almost facing the crowd, but at an angle so they will be in view of the entire audience.

The sheets and comforter will be a sports theme or outdoor hunting version. On the night table is a child's Bible, a box of clay, dry erase pens. A partially licked, sticky, cherry sucker lies next to a small bottle of water. A dry-erase board hangs on his wall near the nightstand, and a B-B gun stands angled in the corner of the room.

The boy is getting ready for bed and already has on his pajama bottoms.

Where the bedroom door would be, will be a chair against the wall with a large T-Shirt hanging off the back.

When the lights go up for this section of the act, the father will act as though he is just entering the boy's bedroom, he will reach over and grab the T-shirt and toss it to his son and the dialogue will begin.

Stage Directions:

The lights slowly rise from darkness to dimness so the audience can see that there is a set on both the right and left of the stage.

No actors are on stage.

Make the lighting for the center stage about 2 clicks above the side sets, enough to signify that the center stage is the main act.

As a gentleman, around the age of 54-64, walks into the room, he places his other smaller glass of milk on the end table.
He positions himself in his chair and continues to eat his brownie with nuts and takes a drink of his milk.
As he sets his glass of milk down on the table, slowly bring up the lights from above, highlighting the main subject. During this settling of the gentleman, bring up the lights slowly…when he reaches for his computer direct the spotlight brightly on him.

The man finishes his brownie and milk and reaches for his laptop computer, opens it, and begins checking his email. After a few minutes, he pauses and, as in deep thought, opens his Microsoft software and begins to type.

ON THE OVERHEAD SCREEN, BRING UP MATT: 6:9 and the title of the play.

"The Lord's Prayer"

He has an online Bible that he often goes to for research and study. He opens it to Matthew 6:9 and begins to read about Jesus teaching the crowd and his disciples "The Lord's Prayer"

He stops reading and puts his head back on the chair, as though the reading triggered a past memory. Pause for 4 seconds.

He changes programs and begins to blog his thoughts.

As he types, the story is shown on a screen above him, as if we are inside the mind of the writer. The story begins complete with the proper pictures as he describes his thoughts.

*(Narrator is off-stage **reading aloud** the older man's thoughts as he types them.)*

Narrator: *(off-stage, reading aloud what the older man is typing.)* **I remember as a young boy, around the age of 12, attending football games with my father. He used to keep the score during the games, and I would be running around playing.**

After the game, my father would take the press box equipment back to the coaches' office in the locker room. Every now and then, I would get to go with him to the locker room. While he was putting away the equipment, I was snooping around trying to admire the 'Big Boy' football players, for I was going to be one someday.

Having come from an athletic family, and my father working full time in the same building as our high school gym, he always had coffee on in his office for all the PE teachers and coaches. Naturally, our family seemed to always be good friends with the coaches and their families.

This one night, as the team did after every game, seemed to be somewhat special to me. There are, at times, even to a 10-year-old, events that are embedded in his memory banks forever. You know those spine- chilling, goose bump memories.

This was one such memory that night… getting to go into the locker room with my father after the high school football games.

(On the screen above the picture of the man writing, a small boy in a hallway with his dad, listening to the head coach speak to his players about the game, is created).

The talk by the coach was not what I remembered, but what will FOREVER be a goose-bump moment...even just thinking about it...was when the coach finished his talk and he asked a senior member of the squad to lead them all in "The Lord's Prayer." This was not such a big thing during the early 1960's, for you see, prayer was still allowed and even encouraged in the public schools.

However, it was the way this captain led the prayer. In a more mature, deep bass voice than what you would expect from a senior in high school, he and the entire football team and coaches began to SING "The Lord's Prayer." The members of the glee club, those who also played football, could be heard above all others and their harmony was bone chilling. Yes, even to this day I still get goose-bumps just thinking about it.

As the gentleman pauses from his writing, he pulls the handle on the side of his chair in the upward direction to raise the footrest.

He gives the impression he will be here for a long time, and leans his head back on the headrest.

He relaxes, his head back, as if looking up in remembrance of this moment. On the screen above, you see and hear a locker room filled with sweaty players in various forms of undress, some still in full uniform...ALL kneeling in reverence to this Prayer and you hear the most beautiful song of men you ever could imagine singing, ***"The Lord's Prayer."***

As the song fades and the screen goes dark, focus the lights on the man in the chair. His head back and his eyes closed as if going to take a nap. Dim the lights slowly…not quite dark, but you can still see the image of the chair and the man.

Scene II

Looking from the crowd onto the stage, the lights are now beginning to brighten on the man's left side of the stage.

(Right front of the stage, viewing standing in front of the stage looking in)
Here is where the father and son walk into the bedroom, the son is shirtless and already in his PJ bottoms. The boy walks ahead of his father and pulls down the covers of his bed. The father is at the door to his room, by the chair next to the nightstand. He reaches over and picks up the T-shirt as the son turns around. The father tosses it to his son and says:

Father: Think fast.

You can see a nightstand next to the young boy's bed and on it is a child's Bible, a box of clay, a dry erase pen and a partially licked, sticky cherry sucker next to a small bottle of water. A dry-erase board hangs on his wall near the nightstand.
The father turns to his son and asks:

Father: Are you ready to say your prayers?

After he has his son ready for bed, they both kneel to say their prayers.

(Optional: In a longer version of this play), could be with the permission of the Country Music Association, the video about a son watching his father pray and then his father listening to his son pray. I think the song is entitled something like, Little Buckaroo by Eddy Arnold), if this version is chosen….as the father and son kneel to pray, the lights dim off them, and the music video would play center stage.

After the video, the focus is on the father and son kneeling beside the bed, ready to pray. Before they start, the little boy says…

Joel: Dad, what was the song those football players were singing in the locker room? It sure sounded awesome.

Father: It was, "The Lord's Prayer," Son.

Joel: What's "The Lord's Prayer, Dad?

Father: It is the prayer that Jesus taught the crowds of people and His Disciples to pray when he was still on Earth teaching and preaching.

Joel: Do you say "The Lord's Prayer, Daddy?

Father: I sure do, Buckaroo…every morning when I get up and every night before I go to bed.

Joel: Can you teach me "The Lord's Prayer," too, Daddy?

The lights go dim as you can see a surprised and unexpected look on the father's face.

The lights are brought back to the man in the recliner. He raises his head as if he has just awakened from a small nap. Still, with his computer on his lap, he begins to adjust his reading glasses and then reaches up, takes his glasses off, and chews on one end of them, as though he has entered deep thought. (Pause for 7 seconds, and then he puts his glasses back on his head), he re-adjusts his computer and begins typing once again.

Narrator: *(off-stage, reading aloud what the older man is typing)* **I can remember that night as though it just happened. I was somewhat unprepared for this young man's deep thoughts. I had to take a moment and regroup our routine. WAS my little hunter, ball player really ready for the adult version of "The Lord's Prayer"? Has he truly outgrown the "now I lay me down to sleep, bless Grandma and every creature under God's dominion" prayer?**

Jesus was 12 when He was preaching in the temple…I had to make a quick decision before he thought I didn't hear him. I think maybe he is ready...God help me make this young man understand the real meaning of this beautiful prayer.

The lights dim center stage and slowly bring up the lights to the father and son bedroom set.

Scene III

There is a silence and a 5-second pause as if the father was a little surprised and unprepared for this question. The father looks at his son, slowly gets up off his knees, and sits on the side of the bed. He picks up his son and sits him on the bed next to him, on his left, closest to the audience. He then reaches over to the nightstand beside the bed and picks up the child's version of the Bible.

Father: Yes, Son, I think maybe you are old enough to learn "The Lord's Prayer."

The father begins to slowly page thru the Bible until he comes to Matthew Chapter 6 verse 9: He looks at his son and points to the scripture. He begins to explain…

Father: Joel, this is a time when Jesus was just beginning His ministry as an adult. People from all over the country had heard of the miracles that Jesus had been accomplishing, like healing the sick, making blind eyes see, and crippled people walk again. So, just think, if you heard of someone doing that today, you'd want to see this man, Jesus, for yourself, wouldn't you?

Joel: Yeah! No kidding!

*The Father and son are sitting on the edge of the bed almost facing the crowd. (as the father begins to explain the prayer to his son, he uses arm gestures to demonstrate his explanation. The father has the son sitting on his left and is holding the Bible with his right hand and pointing to the scriptures with his left index finger.
…like when he says, "Huge crowd gathering" pointing straight out towards the audience, he uses a large animated sweep of his arms from his left to right. When he says, "He chose a spot high on the hill," point to the left side of the stage (straight across from where he is sitting on the side of the bed and up as if pointing to a hillside.)*

Father: So did the people back then. When Jesus saw a huge crowd gathering toward Him, He chose a spot on the side of a hill, high up with His disciples beside Him, and he began to teach them many wonderful ways we are supposed to live. Many of those ways people today have forgotten.

Joel: Like what ways, Dad?

Father: For example, just before he started the lesson on "The Lord's Prayer," he was teaching about humility.

Joel: Hu Mil La DE?

The father sounds out Humility very slowly.

Father: HU Mil La T. That's when Jesus was teaching the crowds and His disciples that when they do a good deed... (pause, thinking of an example... 3 seconds) like when you gave your favorite baseball card to Ryan without asking me or telling me what you had done...you did it in a secret way that only God and Ryan knew. That is what Jesus was talking about... *(pause 2 seconds)* **...do something without bragging about it...like you did. I know it meant a lot to you and you did a good thing...but, that's a different lesson for another night, Son. Tonight, we are going to look at the lesson Jesus gave about how to pray and this has become known as "The Lord's Prayer."**

The father redirects his son's attention to the Bible and begins reading...

Father: Joel, I'll read this one line after another, and you repeat the line after me. You will get a better feeling on how the prayer goes…Ok?

(The father waits for his son to respond)

Joel: uh…ok, Dad

(The father then begins again)

Father: Matt: 6:9, This, then, is how you should pray: 'Our Father who art in Heaven, hallowed be thy name…'

(Father pauses and waits for his son to answer after reading each line)

Joel: My daddy who paints pictures of Heaven, how many know his name?

(The Father takes a backward jerk of his head as if he has just been hit with a sudden, startling, "DID YOU SEE THAT" kind of expression and looks at his son like, 'where did that come from'? (waits for any reaction from the audience to quiet down.)

Father: What did you just say?

Joel: My daddy who paints pictures of Heaven, how many know his name?

Father: How did you get that from what I just read? "Our Father, who art in Heaven, Hallowed be thy name."

Joel: Well...you said Our Father...and you're the only Father I know...except for my 2 Grandfathers and Great Grand Father...

(pauses for 3 seconds, collecting his thoughts, and then begins again)

...and as my only Father, you draw and oil paint pictures of clouds, and I know you're not famous because we don't live in a mansion, and I know your name, but I don't know who else does?

Father: Ok…well that's a new one on me...Let me explain in more detail. In this instance, Jesus was talking about our Heavenly Father…He was praying to "His" father, who still lives in Heaven, and another word for Hallowed is…honored, a Holy name above any other name on Heaven or Earth…

(for a longer musical version of the play...insert a song about Jesus, "No Other Name but Jesus" by Steve Green, Jon Mohr, Bill Gaither, Gary McSpadden.
https://youtu.be/jA43Wf2MYmo
`<iframe width="591" height="360" src="https://www.youtube.com/embed/jA43Wf2MYmo?ecver=1" frameborder="0" allowfullscreen></iframe>`

(Son interrupts his dad's explanation)

Joel: But, Dad…didn't you tell me that Jesus and our heavenly Father were the same person? How could Jesus be praying to Himself?

*(The lights dim with a pause of 8 seconds, bringing the lights back to the man in the chair writing on his computer. As the older man begins to tell the story below, there are home-made videos of time-appropriate stories to follow, as he remembers. Videos of families are being shown on **both side screens** as he types his memory on the **center screen**. We do not want the audience to just sit and listen or read his words on a screen.* ***I suggest that while preparing the script and set, cast members bring personal family videos to be played on the side screens during this scene****. I want them to experience and remember their own parental experiences. Remember: The center screen is typing the older man's memories. Be creative!*

Narrator: *(off-stage, reading aloud what the older man is typing on center screen)* **I was really surprised…ok, shocked when he asked me to explain the Lord's Prayer, and now this was getting deep fast…you never think kids this young ever listen to a word you, or the Sunday school teacher, or preacher says…but then my kids have always been intelligent, deep thinkers and have often caught me off guard with some of the most interesting questions.**

This same little boy, at the great and mighty age of 5, was watching me change the air filter on our worn out old lawn mower. You older adults remember the kind of PUSH MOWERS with a Briggs and Stratton, 3-hp gasoline engine...remember back when gasoline wasn't much over an outrageous price of $0.50. Yes, Fifty Cents a gallon? Boy! Those were the days! Heck, I remember when I bought gas, as a kid mowing yards, for 0.12 cents a gallon and when I turned 16 and bought my first oil guzzling, mosquito killing, 1959 Ford, winged-tipped, tarnished red, Fairlane, BOY, was I proud! Pretty sure it cost me all of $300.00 plus gas.

Anyway, back to my lawn mower story...Joel had watched me remove the filter section of the mower. I, for some reason, needed to go back into the house and get something, when I had come back out...Joel had put the filter back on the mower and began screwing in the long bolt to fasten it down. As sharp as he was at age 5, it really shouldn't have surprised me at his depth of questions at age 10. But like a lot of parents...he never ceased to amaze me with his countless number of questions.

*(As he begins to say the following, show Proverbs 1:2, and the 4 points listed below, on the overhead. **Do not show** 1st Corinthians 12, leave that for the audience to look up)*

Well, there are 4 things I have learned to pray for daily...these 4 are numerously taught throughout the Bible…amazing what you can learn by just doing a single WORD study. Anyway, these 4 items are in the book of Proverbs, and in 1st Corinthians 12, as gifts of the Holy Spirit:

Proverbs 1:2

<u>To know wisdom and instruction;</u>

<u>To discern the words of understanding;</u>

1. To seek after God's Wisdom
2. To seek after God's Knowledge
3. To seek after God's Understanding
4. To seek after God's Discernment

I guess I was going to see just how well those prayers were going to be answered as I tried to explain to a 10-year-old about the understanding of the Holy Trinity.

(Lights begin to fade from the older man and back into the bedroom scene. The son sits on his father's lap looking up at him waiting for a response.)

The father sits, once again, in amazement of the question of his 10-year-old son. He glances around the room as if he were looking for his REAL son... as if the body snatchers had arrived without him knowing it. He then scratches his head with his right hand as if deep in thought.
(This all should take no more than 15 seconds.)

First, he lays the open Bible onto the bed to his right side...He then repositions his son onto the bed beside him (on his left side nearest to the audience). The Father gets up, retrieves his son's dry-erase board, eraser, and red pen. He sits down beside his son and begins to draw out a picture as he explains, to the best of his knowledge, the Trinity to a 10-year-old. As he begins the drawing... (to be included on a separate page attached to back of this play) the same will be displayed on the overhead center screen. We want the audience to feel as if they are sitting on the edge of the bed with the father and son.

Father: Ok, Joel, let's see if I can make this a little less complicated and, by the way, that was a very adult question you just asked. There are many grown-ups still looking for an answer to that question…I am not saying that I have the perfect answer, but I will do my best, as I have come to understand the mystery of the Trinity and OUR FATHER.

(The father begins to draw a line down the middle of the dry erase board. About 4 inches from the top, he draws another line across the board. He then spells out in a vertical row, and does the same format on the other side.)

(You will need a power point presentation to illustrate the drawing on the board.)

Trinity	Tri-Unity
1. God the Father	1. Body
2. God the Son	2. Mind
3. God the Holy Spirit	3. Spirit

As I understand from the book of Genesis 1:26, Then God said, *"Let us"* make man in our image, in our likeness...

He was referring to US as the Father, Son and Holy Spirit, all 3 in one, and THEY created us in THEIR IMAGE and LIKENESS. To me, this means that although there are 3 in one as the Holy Trinity, we are a TRI-UNITY of Body, Mind, and Spirit. We are 3 parts as well, but in one person.

Our body is created in their image and our mind and spirit are in their likeness. Since Adam was the 1st of man to be created, that makes God the father of all mankind...and we fit in that category...right, Bucko?

Does that make any sense at all? ...if not, just remember this drawing, and when you get a little older, perhaps the Holy Spirit will grant you the understanding, Ok? ...are we straight for now? Let's get back to the "Our Father" who art in Heaven?

Joel: Art is when you draw something, right? And you are always drawing or painting, so I just thought you were doing a picture of Heaven.

Father: Ok, so now I understand your thinking. I know I am not a famous artist, and I can be a bit "hallow" once in a while. I will try to make things a little easier from now on...but the word is HALLOWED, and not any resemblance of Halloween...ok?

The word Hallowed, here, means a VERY HOLY Name...a name to honor, respect, and not use in every sentence, or with bad language as you hear so many people do today. The name JESUS, God and Holy Spirit, when understood correctly, will be spoken with very respected understanding...in fact, Joel, ... in the book of Deuteronomy, it states in the 2nd commandment of the 10 commandments...remember we studied the 10 commandments in one of your Sunday School lessons?

Joel: I think so.

*(Show this and all scriptures during this dialog on the 2bedroom overheads. Be creative in using pictures with scriptures...Balance is key...Not too many, and certainly not on every scripture, some **only** scripture...we will discern which ones at an editing session. People will remember a visual more than just hearing or*

seeing a typed message...but not if it is predictable, mix it up.)

Father: In Deuteronomy 5:11 Thou shalt not take the name of the LORD thy God in vain: for the LORD will not hold him guiltless that taketh his name in vain.

Father: That, my son, is a very serious commandment. We really need to remember God's not kidding when he said to NOT with His name in vain……which means, unless you are witnessing, praying, preaching or teaching about Jesus, we should not be uttering His name…especially like we hear so often today…It's just not right….in fact, God commands it!

(In this portion of the dialogue, as the son is sitting to his father's left on the edge of the bed with his legs crossed, and, at times, hanging off the side of the bed…it will be up to the child as to when, for his own comfort, he shifts his weight and positions … so long as he is just far enough away that he can use the arm and motions of a 10-yr-old trying to explain something to an adult.)

Joel: Ok…see if I got it…when we pray "Our Father," we are talking to God, Our Father of all people, and He lives in Heaven, and His name is VERY Holy…right? And we are not to use His name unless we are telling people about Jesus, praying, preaching, or teaching someone about Him. Is that right?

(The father and son exchange a 'high five" with each other)

Father: Give me 5…That's a really good explanation, Son…I'm very proud of you…When did you get so all grown up on me?

(The son shrugs his shoulders and gives one of those "I don't know" looks to his dad)

(As the Father gets up off the bed and puts down the dry erase board on the other side of the bedside table, he most likely needs some blood flow from sitting so long, he says,

Father: Ok, Bucko, let's get on with the "LORDS PRAYER."

He then sits back on the bed next to his son, gives him a left arm hug, and picks up the Bible that is laying on the bed. With his finger, redirects his son's eyes and attention to the next line in the prayer, and then says…

Father: Ok, we have covered…Our Father who is in heaven, Hallowed be thy name...next is: "Thy Kingdom come, Thy will be done, on earth, as it is in Heaven."

(The father raises his hand to his son as if to tell him to wait, don't say a word, then says)

Father: Wait before you say a word. I think it would be a good idea for you to actually see the words instead of leaving it up to your over-active imagination…I have no idea who you might have received that from...must have been your mother.

(The father and son look at each other and just laugh out loud as if they both really know from whom he received his imagination….
The father then, again, redirects his son's eyes to the correct line in the Bible and says...)

Father: Uh...here it is. Ok, you read this to me aloud.

(The son starts re-reading at the beginning, in a mid-tone range, and when he comes to the next line, he speaks in a louder voice.)

Joel: Our Father, who art in Heaven, hallowed be thy name. Thy kingdom come, Thy will be done, on Earth as it is in Heaven...(pause)... Ok, Dad, I have heard you guys say this prayer in church many times but the words never really seem to mean anything...What does Thy Kingdom come, Thy will be done mean?

Father: Thy Kingdom come...The best I can explain it, Son, is that from the beginning of Jesus ministry, He was always trying to teach and prepare the people, and even for us who were born much later, for when Jesus would return to Earth...for when we are in the presence of the Holy Spirit, we are in the midst of the Kingdom of God......

(Interrupting, the son says...)
Joel: But, Dad! Doesn't Jesus live in our hearts when we get saved and ask Him to come live inside us? ...this is all confusing.

Father: You know, you're right...Jesus, the Holy Spirit, and God the Father do live in your Spiritual heart and not your Thumper heart.

I sometimes guess the meaning of the scriptures can seem confusing…that's why God told us that if we really work hard at finding Him with ALL of our Heart, ALL of our mind, and ALL of our Spirit, we would find Him…(pause) Sometimes it is just easier to sit in a pew in church and listen to the preacher talk instead of really getting in and studying for ourselves.

Joel: So, Jesus, the Holy Spirit, and God our Father live in our spiritual hearts? And, also in Heaven...then Heaven must live inside of us too…right?

Father: That's a good way to understand it…and you will always gain just a little more understanding the more you study God's word…and the part of "Thy will be done, on earth as it is in Heaven," reminds me of the time Jesus was in the Garden praying before He was betrayed and turned over to be crucified…

You know, Joel…Jesus could have, at any second, just called out to Heaven and 12,000 Angels would have come and rescued Him from all the pain and suffering that He was about to endure. But he didn't…he prayed to His Father in Heaven and said, "Not my will, but yours be done" Matt 26:39.

So, even though Jesus was still on Earth, He was willing to do what His Father, who is in Heaven, wanted and not what we, on Earth, most often wanted…is this making any sense at all, Son?

Joel: W-e-l-l-l-l-l-l...more so than just reading the words or hearing people say them.

Father: Just remember this lesson and where to go to find the answers. Know where the scripture is located, and when you get older, you will understand it even better...Remember, knowing where to go to find the answers is just as important as to just memorizing a bunch of words.

OK...where were we...here, are you ready to read or use that imagination of yours?

Joel: I'll read. "Our Father who is in Heaven, Hallowed be thy name. Thy Kingdom come, Thy will be done, on Earth, as it is in Heaven…here we are…Give us this day, our daily bread" … (pause 4 seconds) Daily Bread? Do we have to eat bread every day? Oh boy…I love bread!

Father: ME TOO! Bread is one of my favorite meals… (they both laugh)

However, I don't think this is exactly talking about dinner rolls…it means more like when Moses lead the Israelites out of Egypt into the desert on their way to the promised land…they didn't have any grocery stores to buy food as they traveled across the desert. Even though they kept complaining, God still gave them brand new food to eat every day...except for Saturdays, then He gave them enough for two days, so they wouldn't have to work on the Sabbath. Not one day did all the millions of people ever go hungry. The food God provided for them was called 'manna.' It was sort of like our bread, only a whole lot healthier. So, when we say provide for us our 'daily bread,' we really mean our Daily NEEDS, not our wants or greed.

Joel: Does that mean no more Christmas gifts or birthday gifts?

Father: No! No! Son, surprises are a good thing every now and then. God gave us His best gift when He gave us Jesus, so that Whosoever would believe in Him, SHOULD NOT perish. (John 3:16) …so Gifts are a GOOD THING!

Joel: Geeze Loueezzze! That was a close one…. What's next? …your turn to read, Dad.

Father: I was wondering if I got a turn or not.

(Turning back to the open pages, the father uses his right index finger to look for the spot where they left off).

Father: Here we are…back on the road again. Oh, this one is a tough one, Joel…Of all the lessons in life, I think this is one of the hardest I have had to work on. Ouch! It even hurts sometimes to just read it.

Joel: You want me to read it for you?

Father: No that would be taking the easy way out…I guess I needed this lesson more than you…Ok here goes. "And forgive us our debts AS we forgive our debtors."

Joel: So, why is that so hard, Dad?

Father: Well, Son, when you really stop to think about what Jesus is saying…I mean really understand it…well…It means that Jesus will only forgive us of our wrong doings to the degree we forgive others who do us wrong.

Joel: WHAAAAT? I just figured all we had to do was just ask for forgiveness, and our SIN board was wiped clean.

Father: That's true for our salvation, Son. When we truly repent, our sin board IS wiped clean, and we get a new beginning. Unfortunately, most people believe as you stated, that mouthing the words is all that you need to do…but, let's look just a little closer at what Jesus taught his disciples.

(Turning to the book of Mark, Chapter 11: 25-26, the father uses his index finger, starting at the top of Mark 11, and acting if he is scanning down the page to find this scripture.)

Father: Remember, son...this is still JESUS teaching on the hillside...but, this is what the apostles understood hearing. It sure makes one stop to think a lot more about just forgiving from our head instead of our heart. For it's not the words we say that count...it's the truth of how we feel in our heart that concerns "OUR FATHER." If you don't learn anything else from this lesson on how to pray...PLEASE! Learn how to forgive from your heart...Ok, Joel? Remember these are the words of JESUS. Matt 18:35, So likewise shall my Heavenly Father do also unto you, if you from your HEARTS Forgive not everyone his brother their trespasses.

(The father hesitates in mild surprise. He points to the reference with his right index finger and gives his son a slight left elbow to get his attention.)

Father: Here look at this reference to Mark, Chapter 11, verse 25-26.

Mark 11: 25-26 And when ye stand praying, forgive, if ye have aught against any: that your Father, also which is in Heaven, may forgive you your trespasses. 26 But if ye do not forgive, neither will your Father which is in Heaven forgive your trespasses.

Joel: GEEEZZZ... I didn't know Jesus was so serious about the forgiving part...it really must be important.

Father: I think it may be more than just important...I think it's more of a command. Kind of like Jesus is saying, "My way or the highway, Jack. If I'm going to have to go through what I am for your sins to be forgiven, then forgiving each other is the least you can do."

Father: Joel…for years as an altar boy…I was personally requested by the Bishop, for my steady hands, to hold the book of prayers so he could read during Mass…

*(The father takes the Bible and holds it in front of him like he would hold it so someone else could read from it…then moving it around in a playful way, *as to show why having a steady hand was a good thing for an altar boy…then placing it back on his lap, he starts to explain more. * **this gives the actors an opportunity to move around**.)*

I always felt a closeness to God and, at one time, I seriously considered going into the priesthood. I have recited The Lord's Prayer since I started 1st grade…but it wasn't until I started studying the Bible for myself and not just reading it, or listening to someone else give a sermon…For me, son…this really woke me up in my Christian Life. I guess we all have our weaknesses, but I pray God gives me His Grace and Mercy to help me get to where I need to be. I pray the same for you every night.

Joel: Wait a minute, Dad...you mean you have weaknesses? I thought you were awfully strong for an old man!

(Lights go dim on the right side of the stage and back to the man in his chair.)

Narrator: *(off-stage, reading aloud what the older man is typing)* **Now that was a low blow... I must have been all of 36 years old and thought myself to still be in pretty good athletic form...why, just ask me. In my mind, I could still run a 100-yd. dash in 10 seconds; however, my body even laughed at me. I'd be lucky to do a 100yd. dash in 30 seconds in a golf cart. In fact, one night a couple of years after graduating from high**

school and running a 10 sec, 100-yd. dash, a classmate and I got into a discussion…heck, it was an argument… about being able to run the same times we did just a couple of years ago in track. He was a 2 miler, what did he know about sprints? Anyway, it got down to the…put up or shut up…so he had a stopwatch in his car, and we headed to the track. It was a summer evening, and at this age, I always kept my, bat, balls, golf clubs, running shoes, etc. in my car. I was prepared for any game. Anyway, we went to the track, and the best I could do was 11.5…of course it was in street shorts and tennis shoes...YEAH! I had to laugh about that one too…yet in my mind I can still run that 100-yd. dash in 10 seconds. Anyway, I could still hit a fastpitch softball!

I sure miss those trying days, or at least some of them. I don't miss having to work 3 jobs trying to make ends meet. The only thing that met was me, coming and going. I must have had at least 2 or 3 burnouts during the first 10 years of our family.

I can remember coming in from a night shift at 5:am and going to my daughter's baby bed. Shawnna must have been all of 6 months old…I'd pick her up just to hold her, rock her, and pray over her. I did the same for Joel and Ashley when they were born. Yet, none of them ever batted an eyelash and never knew their daddy did such a thing.

It had to be the rocking chair, for I know it wasn't my singing or composing a poem of thankfulness that kept them asleep…Gee, I always thought if I had a way to record my thoughts when I first had them, I'd have written some pretty good stuff…but as usual, by the time I finished time with my special gift from

God and put my baby down, then remembered what words of rhythm and rhyme that had just crossed my mind… the moment had passed.

I realize now that it was just a special moment between God, my child and me not to be shared for fame. Yes, a special moment. How we, as young parents, do not realize until years later, just how special those moments would turn out to be.

(The man pauses and leans his head back in his chair as the lights dim from center stage to the right side again. Remember, all this time, the mother is on the left side of the stage tending to her daughters, getting them ready for bed. The lights on the left side are just enough to let the audience know that they are there, but not enough to distract from the main scene.

The father exchanges playful blows with his son for his wisecrack. He then begins speaking in an exaggerated comic tone of an old, old man)

Father: *I'll tell you what, Sonny...you just put up your dukes, and I'll show you weak for an old man. Well, I'll give you the "what for." You Little Whippersnapper!*

(The father regains his composure and redirects his son's attention to the Bible)

Father: Ok, big guy...any more questions before we move on to the next verse?

Joel: Yeah... OLD MAN...tell me, what did the prayer mean by debtors...I understand trespasses, I think...isn't it like the signs posted when we go hunting, "NO TRESPASSING"? We are not supposed to cross the fence?

Father: Yes, Son...just like it, only different.

(The son and father give each other that "deer in the headlight" look and stare at one another with a fun, surprised look.)

Joel: Say that again!

Father: Just like it, only different? Sounds funny, doesn't it...but it is just like no trespassing signs when hunting...we are not supposed to cross certain marked boundary lines, or we could get into some deep trouble with the landowner. That's why the correct thing to do is always asking permission from the owner before hunting on his property.

We all have our own personal fences and boundary lines we don't allow or want, anyone to cross without our permission. Sometimes WE forget to ask permission… or accidentally on purpose… I mean, or on purpose, do or say something to hurt someone's feelings, property

or private areas of their life. When we do so, we commit a trespass and/or, we then owe a debt of forgiveness to that person. Then again, we are to forgive those who hurt our feelings, property or harm us. Debt, debtors or trespasses they all mean the same thing…

(the father turning quickly to Luke 6:28 and shows him what the Bible says)

Father: Look in Luke…say that 3 times fast. These, too, are the very words of Jesus in the book of Luke chapter 6:27-28.

27 But I say unto you which hear, love your enemies, do good to them which hate you, 28 Bless them that curse you, and pray for them which despitefully use you.

Father: Perhaps that's what makes it so hard for us men, because if someone tries to hurt me, I'm just as apt to punch him in the nose and then ask for his forgiveness. Perhaps we all still have some spiritual growing to do. I will love them from a good distance and pray for them who intentionally want to say and spread rumors about me. That way, I won't be so apt to do something my human nature hasn't perfected yet, but that's getting off the subject just a bit...like I said, Son...this is a hard one for me.

Narrator: *(off-stage, reading aloud what the older man types)* **HARD! Well, that was the understatement of my life. Little did I know just how hard it was going to be in my future years. God really knows how to turn up the heat and, sadly to say, so does that ole' devil. Looking back...well let's not...suffice to say that I sure would like to have back a bunch of those immature, misspoken words that flew out of my**

mouth…and sometimes even to MY surprise! Personal hurt, pain, and rejection seem to bring the worst out in me, and God knows I've had my share, and I swear, half of someone else's. I'll have to ask God when I get to Heaven if, perhaps, some angels went to sleep and forgot to pass a little of this pain, hurt and rejection around. LOL! Life happens, and along the way, we do learn to forgive or we get bitter. Yeah! As my wise ole grandfather used to say, "Get better or get bitter". It's sad that so many of us get bitter before we learn to get better…but! ...God has a way to get our attention…yeah...sooner or later…sooner or later...we learn forgiveness.

(The writer leans his head back against his chair as if, going back into the memory banks of his mind. Once again, the lights are shifting. All this time you can see just enough of the mother rocking her baby and putting her in her baby bed and reading a book to her other daughter, while dad is teaching and tucking in his son)

(The son begins to show signs of getting sleepy and snuggles up just a little closer to his dad. The father puts his left arm around him, welcoming the closeness. Then the father begins to close the lesson by continuing to read the next verse.)

Father: It's getting late isn't it, Son? Let's wrap up this lesson by reading the last part…I think you will understand it pretty well, and won't have so many questions. I can see the day is catching up with the both of us……Verse 13…

(The father reads it to himself silently, as if to make sure of where he left off the last verse. He then repeats…verse 13 out loud)

Father: Hmmmmm…Verse 13…I think everyone has this problem.

Joel: What problem, Dad? *(said in a sleepy voice)*

Father: It say's…Lead us NOT into temptation, BUT deliver us from evil.

Joel: I understand the temptation part…it's hard to walk past those fresh-baked, warm, double chocolate chip cookies, that Mom baked today, without snatching one to see if they were good enough for the rest of you guys to eat…but a little voice inside me said, "I'd better not" …or was that Mom yelling from the other room?

(both father and son give a hardy, but sleepy chuckle)

Father: Yeah, I know…you was just thinking of our health right…Joel? I know for myself there is something, in some way, always ready to test my weaknesses…everyday! What always seemed to catch my eye on this verse was the second part, when Jesus said… "BUT deliver us from evil," it seemed to me that it was like Jesus already knew we would, at some time or another, fall to our temptations and fall into the hands of our spiritual enemies. So, he added an insurance policy at the end. "BUT deliver us from evil," and in verses 14 and 15, to show you how important this part of the prayer is…Jesus, AGAIN, says, 14 For if you forgive men when they sin against you, your heavenly Father will also forgive you. 15 But if you do not forgive men their sins, your Father will not forgive your sins. It's as if Jesus didn't think they understood it the first time. He was teaching them how to pray…He said it for a 2nd time in the same lesson.

(By this time, the son is beginning to fade and starting to slump over onto his father's lap and the Bible. The Father gently pulls him up just enough to be able to put the Bible down behind him at the foot of the bed.

The father starts to hum the song, The Lord's Prayer, that he heard in that football locker room years ago. As he gets up off the bed, while holding onto his sleepy son, he turns toward the bed and repositions his son so that his head is on his pillow. He then helps his son put his legs under the half turned down covers. As he is finishing tucking in his son, his humming is beginning to get a little louder.

To the other side of the stage, you can see the mother about the same time as the father, putting the book down from reading to her daughter and mirroring the fathers moves as she tucks in her daughter. She, too, begins, in unison with the father, to hum The Lord's Prayer song. As the father and mother, at the same time, kiss the heads of their respectful child, the mother kisses her right index and middle fingers as she walks over to the baby crib and gently touches her baby's head.

While the mother is delivering her baby a good night kiss, the FATHER is standing at the side of his son's bed just staring at him...the Father begins to softly sing The Lord's Prayer out loud...the mother still humming about the same tone as the father.

The Father is singing at the time the mother is walking to the baby crib. He is looking down at his son, turning away from his son's bed and walking toward his bedroom door. When he gets to the part of the song, "hallowed be thy name," the mother is turning away from the crib toward the center stage, as if walking out of the bedroom.

REMEMBER, the mother and father are mirroring their moves. The father also turns from his son's bed toward the stage and begins to slowly walk toward the center stage. EACH step he and the mother take toward the center stage, his singing of "THE LORD'S PRAYER gets louder and louder. This is to be timed with meeting his wife at the center of the stage, facing each other in front of the man sitting in his chair with his head leaned back. This should be in proportion to the stage and the man in the chair, only a shadow compared to the spotlight on the mother and father.

The mother is beginning to sing some low harmony…but the father is the main singer as he remembers his locker room experience.

When the father comes to the end of the song…but deliver us from evil…They both grasp each other's hand, looking into each other's eyes, and slowly turn towards the audience and joins in singing…sending spine-tingling chills up the backs of the audience….)

For Thine is the Kingdom, and the Power, and the Glory forever!   Aaaaaaaaamen~!

(The choir behind the scenes, or in the pit, joins in a repeat of the last line as the Holy Spirit fills them and leads them to finish.)

(As the choir is singing, the mother and father walk off the stage as if leaving the room. The choir will repeat the last verse two or three times. (?) As the parents fade into the background, the lights begin to slowly redirect to the man in the chair)

For Thine is the Kingdom, and the Power, and the Glory forever!   Aaaaaaaaamen~!

As the choir is fading out, the man in the chair begins to sit up as if coming out of his slumber. He repositions himself in his chair and begins to type. As he types, the audience will see on the overhead, each letter being typed slowly.

DECEMBER 6^{TH,} 2007
THANK YOU JESUS!

December 6^{th,} 2007…Thank you, JESUS!

5 things for which I am thankful today!

1. My Lord and Savior Jesus Christ
2. My Faith
3. The Creativity the Holy Spirit has loaned me
4. My 3 Children
5. My Grand Children…God Bless them all

(The man closes his laptop and positions it on the left arm of the chair. On the right arm are the remote controls for a TV and a closed cell phone.

He slowly gets out of his chair and stands up in front of his chair and reaches for his cell phone. **(Show a hand and a cell phone on the overhead)** *He opens his cell phone lid to check for any missed calls. He then selects the command that would show if there were any calls…scrolls down to "voice mail" where it shows '0' messages. He sadly closes his cell phone lid and mutters a phrase so the audience can hear.*

Father: Forgive them Lord for they know not what they do.

He then slowly walks toward the back of the stage, as if walking off. He turns his back to the audience and begins walking towards the back of the stage. As he walks the path, the lights are still in the dim to medium state…. lighting his path to the two double doors at the back of the stage. As he approaches the doors, a light above the doors comes on slowly, like a motion detector. To the left of the door is an exaggerated blackboard like in a doctor's office telling if someone is in or out of the office. Only this board has on top of it, a title of "VISITORS - TODAY." It is divided into two sides with a line down the middle. On one side, it says YES on the other side, it says NO. Halfway down the board, there is another line drawn across the middle, and under it are the large words, "PHONE CALLS TODAY" and another line under it with the YES and NO labels.

The man picks up the RED dry erase pen and makes a check mark under the two "NO" columns. The audience cannot see the board until he goes thru the double doors and then the spotlight goes to the board. It is also shown on the overhead. The double doors should open and close slowly as the man fades into the background.

This is to signify what many senior citizens experience everyday…forgotten by children, family, and friends.

The sign over the double doors reads in bold letters, **"MENTAL WARD", family only**. *As the man disappears behind the doors, all the lights on stage go dim.*

On the overhead is a video, possibly from U-TUBE, entitled, ***"THE LORD'S PRAYER."***

"The Lord's Prayer" by Bill and Gloria Gaither (Live}
```
<iframe width="591" height="360" src="https://www.youtube.com/embed/fA47_QaSKgY?ecver=1" frameborder="0" allowfullscreen></iframe>
```
https://youtu.be/fA47_QaSKgY

The choir begins to sing, **"For thine is the kingdom, and the power, and the glory forever! Aaaaaaaaamen!**

As an option to make a mental triggering point for the following prayer after the Amen, the spotlight goes to the son's bed…he sits up like he is sleep talking, and says:

Joel: Ahhhmen?…All…..MEN?….ALMOND!...... That's NUTS!

(The son flops back onto his pillow, and the lights on stage go out, and the overhead screen comes on with the following. The **narrator** *will read, as he invites the congregation to join in. Matthew 6:9-15.*

This, then, is how you should pray:

Our Father who art in Heaven,

Hallowed be THY name,

THY kingdom come,

Thy will be done,

on Earth as it is in Heaven.

Give us this day, our daily bread.

Forgive us our debts,

as we forgive our debtors.

And lead us not into temptation,

but deliver us from evil."

For if you forgive men when they sin against you, your heavenly Father will also forgive you. But if you do not forgive men their sins, your Father will not forgive your sins. For thine is the Kingdom and the Power and the Glory forever…

AAAAAMEN!

(The house lights remain in the same position to discourage the audience from getting up and leaving. The lights will come to a medium position on the center of the stage as the minister or playwright comes to center stage.)

Note by the playwright:

At this time, the playwright and/or minister will come out and continue the work of the Holy Spirit and give the opportunity for an ALTAR CALL. The minister will do the altar call or the play will not be a production at his theatre or church facility. I feel that the body of Christ of today is losing the art of ministry.

Nowhere in the Bible did I ever see or hear of JESUS teaching or preaching then saying…if anyone has needs, my apostles and disciples will be down here on the left side of this hill to hear your complaints...Imean needs.

JESUS Always ministered to the people HE Taught. That's why He, at times, needed to go away by Himself and pray so He could get renewed by His Father, for how else would He know what His father in Heaven desired.

I believe Jesus said, and pray that it becomes our desire,

"I only do that which I see my Father doing."

-THE END-

NOTES: